STIRLING
IN
50
BUILDINGS

JACK GILLON

AMBERLEY

First published 2019

Amberley Publishing, The Hill, Stroud
Gloucestershire GL5 4EP

www.amberley-books.com

British Library Cataloguing in Publication Data.
A catalogue record for this book is available from the British Library.

ISBN 978 1 4456 9087 2 (print)
ISBN 978 1 4456 9088 9 (ebook)

Typesetting by Aura Technology and Software Services, India.
Printed in Great Britain.

Contents

Key

1. Stirling Castle
2. The Royal Palace, Stirling Castle
3. The Great Hall, Stirling Castle
4. The Bruce Monument, Castle Esplanade
5. The Star Pyramid and the Drummond Pleasure Garden
6. The Virgin Martyrs Monument and the Valley Cemetery
7. The Church of the Holy Rude, Castle Wynd
8. The Old Grammar School, Castle Wynd
9. Argyll's Lodging, Castle Wynd
10. Mar's Wark, Castle Wynd
11. Cowane's Hospital – The Guildhall, St John's Street
12. Mercat Cross, Broad Street
13. Stirling Tolbooth
14. Town Clerk Norrie's House, Broad Street
15. Darnley's House, Bow Street
16. Stirling Boys' Club, St John Street
17. Bruce of Auchenbowie's House, St John's Street
18. Stirling Old Town Jail, St John Street
19. Former Erskine Church (Marykirk), St John Street
20. The Old High School, Spittal Street/Academy Road
21. Former Spittal's Hospital, Spittal Street
22. No. 53 Baker Street and No. 1 Bank Street
23. John Cowane's House, St Mary's Wynd
24. Atheneum, King Street
25. The Golden Lion Hotel, Nos 8–10 King Street
26. Former Drummond Tract Building, King Street/Murray Place
27. Thistles Shopping Centre
28. The Stirling Arcade
29. Stirling Railway Station, Goosecroft Road
30. The Engine Shed, Forthside Way
31. The Wolfcraig Building and the Stirling Wolf, Port Street/Dumbarton Road
32. The Black Boy Fountain, Allan Park
33. Stirling Town Wall
34. Allan Park South Church
35. Statue of Robert Burns, Corn Exchange Road
36. Stirling War Memorial, Corn Exchange Road
37. Stirling Library
38. Stirling Municipal Buildings
39. Albert Halls
40. Glebe Crescent
41. Stirling Smith Art Gallery and Museum
42. The Beheading Stone, Mote Hill
43. Stirling Old and New Bridges
44. Raploch Community Campus, Drip Road
45. Airthrey Castle
46. The National Wallace Monument, Abbey Craig
47. Cambuskenneth Abbey
48. St Ninians Old Parish Kirk and St Ninian's Tower, Kirk Wynd
49. Battle of Bannockburn Visitor Centre
50. Bannockburn House

Introduction

Stirling, than which there are few towns more distinguished for historical incident, and certainly none more remarkable for beauty of situation, is at least as ancient as any other of our present towns, and unquestionably much older than the most of them. Like the metropolis of its kingdom it is built on an eminence that rises gradually from the east, and is bounded on the west by its veteran fortress, raised on the summit of a high and precipitous rock, and affording from its commanding situation, views of surrounding scenery which for richness and variety are perhaps unsurpassed in any other portion of the world.

A New Description of the Town and Castle of Stirling, 1935

It is chiefly for its antiquities and the interesting historical associations connected with them, together with the singularly delightful circumstances of its situation, that Stirling is remarkable, in the eyes of either the native of Scotland or the foreign tourist.

Picture of Stirling, Robert Chambers, 1830

The first thing probably that will strike the stranger is the contrast that the town presents between the old and the new. Side by side with tramway cars, electric lights, and the most recent developments of sanitary science, he will

View from the castle.

find buildings that take him back into the sixteenth century, and to even earlier periods still. The lower portion of the town and the fine suburbs are largely the creation of the nineteenth century; but the further one moves up the rocky slope towards the Castle, the further back into the centuries does he get. Many of the old houses built for lairds and lords and frequenters or dependents of the Court, in the sixteenth and seventeenth centuries, are still in existence, though now inhabited for the most part by a greatly different class from that for which they were built.

Guide to Stirling in 1911

Geography was a critical factor in Stirling's development. Spanning the boundary between the Highlands and Lowlands, and standing at the heart of Scotland, it was 'the key of the Highlands'. The town developed at the lowest bridging point over the Forth, which was a vitally strategic crossroads, and the location of the rugged volcanic crag of the Castle Rock.

The town grew on the steep tail that runs down from the castle's rocky crag and the early settlement prospered under the protection of the castle. It was one of the four principal royal burghs of Scotland; the most ancient charter of the burgh was granted by Alexander I in 1120. It was the marketplace for Stirlingshire and a port from medieval times.

During the thirteenth and fourteenth centuries, the castle and town were razed during the Wars of Independence between England and Scotland – defensive walls were built around the town in 1547. In the fifteenth and sixteenth centuries, the Stuart kings made Stirling their favoured residence and the arrival of the royal court did much to foster the status of the town, with the nobility building elaborate town houses (lodgings) for convenient attendance at court.

Stirling is central to Scotland and its history, and today, having been granted city status in 2002 as part of the Queen's Jubilee celebrations, it is a thriving city with a proud and distinctive identity, which retains much of its ancient character and a wealth of fine heritage buildings. This has made the task of selecting fifty buildings to represent the best of the city's architecture immensely difficult. The book takes the development of Stirling as its broad theme, and includes buildings which seem to best represent the city's long history. Early books on the town's history, media reports contemporary with events in the town, and a mix of old and new images are the main sources used to chronicle the fifty buildings.

The 50 Buildings

1. Stirling Castle

> The most interesting and important edifice in Stirling is the Castle crowning the precipitous extremity of the ridge on which the town is built, and forming the most conspicuous object to the surrounding country.
>
> *The Merchants' Guide to Stirling*, 1897

Set dramatically on its high crag, Stirling Castle dominates the landscape for miles around. Although there is no clear evidence, it is likely that the naturally defensive site of the castle was a stronghold from prehistoric times. The earliest reference to the castle is in the early twelfth century, when Alexander I endowed a chapel within it. The castle changed hands repeatedly in the wars between Scotland and England.

Most of today's castle buildings date from the time in the late fifteenth to sixteenth centuries when it was a fortress, royal palace and a favourite residence of the Stuart kings. After the Union of the Crowns in 1603, the Stuarts effectively abandoned the castle as a residence. The castle was in use as a military base from the late seventeenth century and additional defences were built in 1708, due to the unrest caused by the Jacobite threat.

The castle is well defended on three sides by steeply sloping rock faces. The approach from the south was more of a soft target and was the most fortified. The present forework dates from around 1506 and was built under the reign of

Stirling Castle.

Stirling Castle.

King James IV. It originally consisted of six towers with conical roofs which, along with the guardhouse, were twice as high as at present.

The national importance and tourism potential of Stirling Castle was recognised in the 1960s and a programme of restoration works were undertaken. The castle is now one of the most visited tourist sites in Scotland.

The King's Knot, within the King's Park, is a significant built landscape feature which is historically closely associated with the castle. The Knot consists of a concentric stepped octagonal mound covered with grass and formed part of a magnificent seventeenth-century formal garden. It was originally the centrepiece of a surrounding rectangular parterre garden which would have been planted with box trees and ornamental hedges. The King's Knot is known locally as the 'Cup and Saucer'. The Queen's Knot is a smaller, less distinct mound within the gardens.

The King's Gardens lie immediately to the south-west of the Castle-hill, and to the south of the Castle. Their present condition is that of a marshy piece of pasture-ground. This interesting monument of the taste of our national sovereigns is completely desolated, so far as shrubs and flowers are concerned. The utmost exertion of the memory of the present generation, can only recollect an old cherry-tree, which stood at the corner of one of the parterres, and which was burnt down by the wadding of a shot, which some thoughtless sportsman fired into its decayed trunk, as he happened to pass it on his way home from the fields. It is yet possible, however, to trace the peculiar form into which the ground had been thrown by its royal proprietors. In the centre, a series of concentric mounds, of a polygonal, but perfectly regular shape, and rising above one another towards the middle, are yet most distinctly visible. An octagonal mound in the centre, is called the King's Knot, and is said, by tradition, to have been the scene of some forgotten play or recreation, which the King used to enjoy on that spot with his court. In an earlier age, this strange object seems to have been called the Round Table; and, in all probability, it was the scene of the out-of-door's game of that name, founded upon the history of King Arthur. To give further countenance to this supposition, we have ascertained the fact that James IV, with whom Stirling was a favourite and frequent residence, was excessively fond of the game of the Round Table, which probably appealed, in a peculiar manner, to his courtly and chivalric imagination.

Picture of Stirling, Robert Chambers, 1830

The gardens were built on the site of the Round Table, which is referred to in a 1530 poem, 'Testament and Complaynt of our Soverane Lordis Papyngo', by Sir David

PORTCULLIS GATE AND PALACE, STIRLING CASTLE.

Above: Stirling Castle portcullis gate and palace.

Left: The King's Knot from the castle.

Lindsay: 'Adieu, fair Snawdoun, with thy towris hie, Thy Chapill – Royal, Park, and Tabill Round'. Stirling had strong associations with King Arthur and it was long claimed that Stirling Castle was the Snowdon of Arthurian legend. The site was used for medieval jousting tournaments 'in the spirit of the Knights of the Round Table, which the courtly personages of former times are known to have been so fond'.

2. The Royal Palace, Stirling Castle

The Palace at Stirling Castle is a quadrangular building, having three ornamental sides presented to the view of the spectator. On each of the ornamented sides there are six recesses, in each of which a pillar rises close to the wall, having a statue on the top. Most of those on the eastern side are mythological figures. On the northern side, the figures are more of this world's kind of beings; the first from the east corner is unquestionably a statue of the royal founder. Above and below the figure there runs a wreathed scroll, which is considered unique. The visitor may derive a very good hour's amusement from the inspection of these curious relics, some of which are valuable as commemorating costumes of former times.

The Tourist's Companion Through Stirling, John Forbes, 1848

The Royal Palace at Stirling Castle was built during the latter part of the reign of James V as appropriately prestigious accommodation for the king and his queen,

The Royal Palace, Stirling Castle.

Above: The Royal Palace, Stirling Castle, from inner courtyard.

Left: The Royal Palace, Stirling Castle – statues.

Mary de Guise. Work started in the 1530s and it was mainly complete at the time of James' death in December 1542. The interior originally consisted of an almost symmetrical arrangement of a matched group of rooms of state: a public outer hall, where nobles and courtiers met the monarch; an inner hall, for more exclusive audiences; and an inner bedchamber for the most elite circle of advisers. Daniel Defoe described them as 'the noblest I ever saw in Europe, both in Height, Length and Breadth'. The rooms were grouped around a paved courtyard known as the Lion's Den – from the heraldic lion of Scotland or possibly from the fact that it housed a real lion. The palace was the childhood home of the young Mary, Queen of Scots.

The palace continued in use as an important royal residence until the Union of the Crowns in 1603, when the court moved to London and the building lost its main purpose. It was gradually converted for military accommodation in the eighteenth century. After the departure of the army in 1964, the building served as a function room and café. In June 2011, the building opened to the public after a £12 million project to recreate its original splendour. This included replicas of a series of the beautifully carved oak portrait roundels, known as the Stirling Heads, which were originally installed on the ceiling of the king's Presence Chamber. The original heads had been taken down in 1777, as they had become insecure.

The exterior of the palace is festooned with around 200 bold carvings, which represent a unique collection of Scottish Renaissance sculpture. A devil, grotesque monsters and a line of armed soldiers face the outside. Classical deities and musicians decorate the inner courtyard. James V (top left in the collage) is depicted in a more natural form with a bushy beard and wearing the Highland dress of the time. They would originally have been painted and gilded, and were designed to proclaim the king's importance. R. W. Billings (1813–74), the Victorian architectural historian, described them as 'the fruits of an imagination luxuriant but revolting'.

3. The Great Hall, Stirling Castle

The Great Hall was completed in 1503, in the reign of James IV. It was intended as a magnificent venue for royal occasions and is the largest and finest medieval hall in Scotland, requiring five fireplaces to heat it. The hall was used for the baptisms of James VI in 1566 and Prince Henry in 1594. The banquet following the christening of Prince Henry was a lavish affair with a huge boat floating in an artificial sea, dispensing sweetmeats and equipped with working cannons for a salute to the young prince. The hall was very occasionally used for sittings of parliament.

After the Union of the Crowns in 1603, the hall was no longer required for its original ceremonial uses and it was radically adapted by the military. Since the army moved out in the mid-1960s, the hall has been the subject of a major

The Great Hall, Stirling Castle.

restoration scheme which has returned it to close to its original condition. This included the renewal of the spectacular hammer-beam roof and the controversial golden yellow limewash. The restored Great Hall was opened by Queen Elizabeth II on 30 November 1999.

4. The Bruce Monument, Castle Esplanade

The esplanade in front of the castle entrance was built in 1812 and 'commands magnificent views of some of the fairest and most historic scenes in Scotland'. The massive 11-foot- (3.3-metre) high statue of Bruce on the Castle Esplanade depicts the Warrior King looking towards Bannockburn and sheathing his sword in 'the moment of victory'. The inscription on the monument reads: 'King Robert the Bruce: June 24th, 1314' – the date of the Battle of Bannockburn.

The statue was paid for by public subscription, sculpted by Andrew Currie (1812–91) and unveiled on 24 November 1877 by Lady Alexander of Westerton in the presence of dignitaries, Scottish regiments and an immense crowd of spectators. When the statue was unveiled, 'the hero of Bannockburn stood out in bold relief, the face expressing conscious dignity, and the whole figure manly bearing and great courage. The vast assemblage burst into loud cheers, which were followed by a royal salute of cannon from the ramparts of the Castle.'

The Bruce Monument, Castle
Esplanade.

On the north side of the cemetery stands a pyramidal emblem in stone of the
permanence of Scripture. The building, which was erected by one of Stirling's
most generous sons - Mr. William Drummond - is not less curious-looking than
imposing; and, in addition to a formidable array of hieroglyphic signs, displays
a variety of biblical quotations. Down in the valley are many interesting, though
less striking objects; a pretty pond, a tasteful water-fountain, and several fine
statues of Scotch martyrs.

The History of Stirlingshire, William Nimmo, 1880

As the name suggests, William Drummond (1793–1868), Stirling's prolific
benefactor, was responsible for the Pleasure Ground, which is the setting for
the Star Pyramid. Drummond was a prominent Stirling businessman who is
described as a 'seedsman, evangelist and an ardent Presbyterian'. He was the
brother of Peter Drummond (1799–1877), the founder of Stirling's Drummond

Above: The Star Pyramid.

Below: The Star Pyramid and William Drummond's sarcophagus.

Tract Enterprise. The Pleasure Ground was laid out in 1863 as a setting for the Star Pyramid, the largest pyramid structure in Scotland. The pyramid is dedicated to the cause of the Presbyterian Church in Scotland; it also publicised his brother's Drummond Tract Enterprise. The pyramid form was popular at the time as a symbol of stability and endurance. William Drummond's massive polished grey granite sarcophagus, inscribed 'Born 14 February 1793 Died 25th November 1888', stands next to the pyramid.

6. The Virgin Martyrs Monument and the Valley Cemetery

> Immediately beneath the castle esplanade to the south, lies the town cemetery. The scene, while full of impressive loveliness, is also very deceptive. From the natural beauty of the situation, and the exquisite skill with which statuary, shrubbery, and rockeries are arranged throughout the burial garden, it is hard to be convinced that what is seen is for the most part artificial.
>
> *The History of Stirlingshire*, William Nimmo, 1880

The Virgin Martyrs Monument in the Valley Cemetery depicts an angel watching over two young girls, with the older of the two reading the Bible to the other.

The Virgin Martyrs Monument.

Above and below: The Valley Cemetery.

It commemorates two young Wigtownshire girls, Margaret and Agnes Wilson, who were sentenced to death by drowning in 1685. The girls were Covenanters and refused to swear an oath of allegiance to Charles II, which amounted to them committing high treason. Agnes, who was in her early teens, had her sentence commuted. However, Margaret, who was aged eighteen, along with an elderly neighbour, Margaret McLaughlin, were tied to stakes on 11 May 1685 in the Solway Firth and left to drown in the incoming tide. The monument was erected in 1859 and the cupola was added in 1867. The sculptor was Alexander Handyside Ritchie (1804–70) and the cupola was by John Rochhead, the architect of the National Wallace Monument.

> We know of no sweeter cemetery than that of Stirling.
>
> William Wordsworth

The Valley Cemetery was laid out in 1857–58 by Peddie & Kinnear as an extension to the kirkyard of the Church of the Holy Rude. It was previously an important open space between the castle and the town where jousting and public events, such as horse markets, were held. The rocky outcrop that overlooks the cemetery is known as the Ladies' Rock and formed an elevated vantage point for the ladies of the court to view the royal tournaments – it continues to provide panoramic views across to the Trossachs and Ben Lomond.

The creation of the Valley Cemetery was due to the Revd Charles Rogers. Rogers was chaplain at the castle and a town councillor. He was said to have had a degree of statue mania – he was responsible for the Wee Wallace on the Atheneum, Bruce on the esplanade, the Martyrs Monument and the statues of the heroes of the Scottish Presbyterian Reformation (John Knox, Andrew Melville, Alexander Henderson, James Renwick, James Guthrie, and Ebenezer Erskine) in the Valley Cemetery. The cemetery was largely funded by William Drummond.

7. The Church of the Holy Rude, Castle Wynd

The Church of the Holy Rude is the original parish church of Stirling and one of Scotland's most important medieval buildings. A church was first established on the site in 1129 during the reign of David I (1124–53). Between 1371 and 1390, King Robert II dedicated an altar to the Holy Rude (Holy Cross) within the church and it became known as the Holy Rude. The original church was destroyed, along with much of Stirling, in a devastating fire in 1405. The new church with its distinctive square belfry tower was rebuilt from 1414.

In the medieval period, the Scottish burghs generally contained only one parish church, which was central to the life of the community. It was accordingly of significant scale and splendour, with chapels and adornments added by the trade guilds and private individuals.

The Church of the Holy Rude.

The church is closely associated with the monarchy. It was the venue for the coronation of Mary, Queen of Scots, on 9 September 1543 and the hastily arranged coronation of her son, the infant James VI, on 29 July 1567, after his mother was forced to abdicate. It is the only church in the United Kingdom, apart from Westminster Abbey, still used for public worship to have hosted a coronation.

The church was restored in the late 1930s, when the partition that had divided the building into two places of worship was removed.

The walls of the church show signs of musket shot and cannon fire from battles around the Castle.

8. The Old Grammar School, Castle Wynd

The earliest note of a Grammar School in Stirling is under the date 1173, and continuously from that date such was carried on with considerable success by reason of the authorities bestowing not a little attention on its affairs, and successions of apt and qualifeit doctouris having been appointed to the oversight.

Auld Biggins of Stirling, William Drysdale, 1904

The Old Grammar School.

The building now occupied by the Portcullis Hotel was built in 1788 as Stirling's Grammar School. It was built on the site of an earlier Grammar School, which dated to 1470. There are records of a school in Stirling dating back to the twelfth century. The Grammar School was the 'chief seat of learning in the burgh' until the opening of the High School in 1854. The building closed in 1856 and was used as a store by the Stirlingshire militia for a time before its conversion for hotel use.

9. Argyll's Lodging, Castle Wynd

On the other side of the Wynd is a building of much architectural merit, an examination of which will well repay the time spent on it. It dates from 1632, and is certainly the finest specimen of the architecture of that period to be found in the district. It was built by Sir William Alexander of Menstrie, afterwards Earl of Stirling, poet, courtier, and statesman, and the crest and motto over the doorway are his. After his death, in 1640, the house became the property of the Earl of Argyll. Hence the name of Argyll's Lodging, by which it has ever since been known. Argyll made considerable additions—said by experts to be not in quite so good taste as the original—to the building, and sprinkled the walls liberally with the boar's-head crest of the family. The property was held by the Argylls till well on in the eighteenth century, and then passed through several hands, till, just about a hundred years ago, it was purchased by the Government and converted into a military hospital. Argyll's Lodging, besides affording house room to its proprietors when required, has had its royal residents. It was occupied by Charles II, when he was here in 1650 endeavouring to regain the throne his father had lost. The last royal personage who spent a night under its roof was the Duke of Cumberland, in 1746, who rested here, in his pursuit of Prince Charlie, till the bridge was sufficiently repaired to allow him and his army to resume their northward march. He also was presented with the freedom of the burgh—the tickets for him and the Prince of Hesse being delivered in silver boxes richly made and gilded —perhaps to cover the facility with which the Magistrates had admitted the rebel prince into the town.

A Guide to Stirling in 1911

Argyll's Lodging is the most important and complete surviving seventeenth-century town house in Scotland. It sits behind a screen wall with a rusticated entrance gateway on Castle Wynd, on the final approach to the castle.

The lodging was developed from a small sixteenth-century house in a number of phases and by a number of owners. In 1629, Sir William Alexander was the new owner and had the house enlarged and remodelled. Sir William was involved in the settlement of Nova Scotia and an armorial tablet on the wall above the main entrance displays Alexander's coat of arms with the shield supported by a Native American. Scrolls show his family motto, *Avt Spero Avt Sperno*, and the motto of Nova Scotia, *per mare per terras*.

Argyll's Lodging.

Argyll's Lodging.

Archibald Campbell then bought the house and made significant enlargements and alterations: the courtyard was enclosed behind a screen wall and an elaborate entrance gate installed. In 1764, the 4th Duke of Argyll sold the house and it remained in domestic use until 1800 when it was purchased by the army for use as a military hospital. It became a youth hostel in 1964. In 1996, it was restored to its former historic splendour and opened as a museum.

1c. Mar's Wark, Castle Wynd

The house of the Earl of Mar is almost the only one of the private palaces of that age, now surviving in any shape. It faces down Broad Street, from any part of which it must have had, when entire, a fine appearance. It was, originally, a quadrangular building, with a small court in the centre. We are now only left the ruins of the front of the square.

A Picture of Stirling, Chambers, 1830

At the head of Broad Street stand the remains of the house built by the Earl of Mar, or Mar's Work. In the centre of its front are the royal arms of Scotland, and on the projecting towers on each side those of the Regent Mar and his countess, all in a fine state of preservation. The stones were brought from the ruins of

Cambuskenneth Abbey, the extreme dilapidation of which is thus accounted for. Some trifling inscriptions are still legible upon the lintels of the doors and windows; and what still remains of the fabric serves to protect the street and market-place from the fury of the west winds.

The Tourist's Companion Through Stirling, John Forbes, 1848

The proximity to the castle made Castle Wynd one of the most significant parts of the town and a number of Stirling's most noteworthy historic buildings were built in the area: Mar's Wark, Argyll's Lodging and the Church of the Holy Rude.

Part of the elaborate front façade of Mar's Wark, which dominates the top of Broad Street, is all that remains of the once splendid town mansion of John Erskine, Earl of Mar. Mar's Wark, or Lodging, was commissioned in around 1569 by the influential Erskine, hereditary Keeper of Stirling Castle and one-time Regent of Scotland. The façade features an abundance of sculptures with the royal armorial bearings of Scotland over the entrance and the Erskine family heraldic panels on the two flanking towers.

Mar's Wark.

Above left and right: Castle Wynd and Mar's Wark.

Much of the stone used in the construction of Mar's Wark was salvaged from Cambuskenneth Abbey. The rhyming inscriptions on the building have been interpreted as either 'offensive effrontery' or aimed at 'disarming the criticism' that might have arisen due to the source of the building materials:

I pray all luikaris on this luging, with gentile E to gif thair juging.
I pray all lookers on this lodging, with gentle eye to give their judging.

The moir I stand on oppin hitht. My faultis moir subject ar to sitht.
The more I stand on open height, my faults more subject are to sight.
(I am conspicuous, so my mistakes are more apparent)

Mar's Wark was converted into barracks after the 1715 Jacobite rebellion and was badly damaged during the 1746 siege of the castle. The building ended its life rather ignominiously as the town workhouse. The lodging itself was subsequently used as a quarry for other building projects. It is said that the only reason that it survived in any form was due to the fact that it sheltered the marketplace from the winds whistling down Broad Street.

The older image shows Mar's Wark in a more complete state with conical roofs on the octagonal towers.

11. Cowane's Hospital – The Guildhall, St John's Street

John Cowan, a merchant in Stirling, between the years 1633 and 1637, left forty thousand merks, to endow a hospital, or alms-house, for twelve decayed brethren of the guild or mercantile corporation of Stirling. The money was invested in the purchase of lands, which now yield a revenue of upwards of £3,400 sterling per annum. From this fund about a hundred and forty persons, at present, receive relief. The front of the house exhibits a full length statue of the founder, which will be looked upon with interest as a memorial of the costume of the better order of Scottish burghers, in the reign of Charles I.

A Picture of Stirling, Chambers, 1830

The distinctive Cowane's Hospital was built between 1637 and 1648 as an almshouse for destitute members of the merchant guild. It was funded by a bequest in the will of John Cowane (1570–1633), a prosperous Stirling merchant. The building was reconstructed as a Guildhall in 1852.

In the 1660s, the grounds were designed with ornamental gardens and, in 1712, Thomas Harlaw, gardener to the Earl of Mar, laid out a bowling green, which is one of the earliest in Scotland. The cannons in the grounds were captured at Sebastopol during the Crimean War.

Over the entrance to the Guildhall is a niche with a statue of John Cowane and the inscriptions: 'This Hospital was erected and largely provyded by John Cowane,

Cowane's Hospital.

Cowane's Hospital.

Above left: Cowane's Hospital plaque.

Above right: Cowane's Hospital, Auld Staneybreeks.

Deane of Gild, for the Entertainment of Decayed Gild Breither. John Cowane, 1639.' and 'I was hungrie and ye gave me meate, I was thirstie and ye gave me drinke, I was a stranger and ye tooke me in, naked and ye clothed me, I was sicke and ye visited me. Matt. xxv. 35.' The statue of John Cowane is known as *Auld Staneybreeks* (old stone-trousers). There is a local legend that every Hogmanay, *Auld Staneybreeks* gets down for a dance in the courtyard.

At the time of writing, the building is closed due to deterioration of the building fabric. However, Heritage Lottery funding has been allocated for repairs and conversion into a visitor attraction.

12. Mercat Cross, Broad Street

Broad Street, anciently named Hiegait, and afterwards High Street, was once the market and chief place of business in Stirling. Here were the Tolbooth, the Mercat Cross and the Tron. It was here also the weekly markets and annual fairs were held, stances being allotted to the various trades, whose wares were exposed on *staiks* or stalls. During the sixteenth century, this spacious street contained the *ludgings*, or mansions, of the noblemen and Church dignitaries attached to the Court during the Royal residence in the Castle. The principal municipal officials had also their residences in the street.

The Merchants' Guide to Stirling, 1897

In the centre of Broad Street stands the restored Market Cross of the burgh. The original Cross—of unknown antiquity, but supposed to date from the thirteenth century—was, along with the Tron, which stood a little higher up, removed in 1792, as it was considered an obstruction to the traffic and a danger to the lieges from its ruinous condition. Only the unicorn, which surmounted the ancient pillar, was preserved. As there is now plenty of room for all the traffic that finds its way through the Broad Street, the time was propitious for the re-erection of this old landmark. Accordingly in 1891, Mr. Robert Yellowlees, then Provost of the Burgh, had the whole Cross restored to its ancient form and appearance— as nearly as the remaining descriptions of it and the advice of experts could determine—and generously presented the structure as a gift to the town.

A Guide to Stirling in 1911

Market Crosses are generally placed in some open square or broad streets in the towns where they are situated, to mark the spot where the markets are held. They are also used to publish edicts of a royal or burghal nature. They were also used as a place of punishment for offenders against the burghal laws, for a place of meeting for the inhabitants to celebrate any naval or military victory, and to burn any proclaimed books and papers. In the burgh records, we find that our old Cross was used for all these purposes. On 23 October, 1692, it was used as the place from which to issue a proclamation for securing the peace of the kingdom. On April 16, 1689, it was used to proclaim their Majesties, King William and Queen Marie, with all solemnity. In 1714, it was used for the more commercial use of regulating the time of sale of fish, butter, cheese, and fowls.

The Stirling Antiquary, W. B. Cook, 1893

Mercat crosses were a symbol of a town's right to hold a market, an important privilege. It marked the spot where trade was carried out and public proclamations were made. In 1792, the mercat cross was removed from a central position on the street to ease traffic movement. It was reinstated and was unveiled on 23 May 1891, which 'evoked much interest and enthusiasm for the community at large'. The reinstated cross was noted as being 'in its design and general aspect a faithful reproduction of that taken down'.

The Stirling mercat cross consists of an octagonal shaft on a stepped circular base and is surmounted by a unicorn (known as the Puggy) with a lion rampant and St Andrew's Cross. Only the Puggy, 'a mute witness to many strange, tragic and romantic events', dates from the original mercat cross.

Broad Street.

Above left: Unveiling of the Mercat Cross in 1891.

Above right: The Puggy.

13. Stirling Tolbooth

The original Tolbooth was erected around 1473 and was partially rebuilt in 1563 due to its dangerous condition. It was taken down and rebuilt, with the addition of the steeple, in 1703–05 according to *ane drauglit or sceme* prepared by Sir William Bruce of Kinross.

The street at the front of the Tolbooth was one of the places where wrongdoers were executed or otherwise punished. A small plaque on the Tolbooth commemorates the brutal public execution of John Baird and Andrew Hardie on 8 September 1820. Baird and Hardie were activists involved in the Radical War or Scottish Insurrection – a period of strikes and conflict in which workers demanded a more representative government, the end to economic depression and fair wages. The authorities feared the kind of revolutionary turmoil that had been seen in France some decades earlier and were intent on the ruthless suppression of the rebellion.

On 5 April 1820, Baird and Hardie were the leaders of a small group of Radicals that was marching on Carron Ironworks near Falkirk with the intention of seizing weapons. They were apprehended by government troops near Bonnybridge, along with a number of others, and imprisoned at Stirling Castle. Tried and found guilty of treason, they were sentenced to be hanged and beheaded. The grim execution took place in front of the Tolbooth. It seems that the Stirling hangman refused to carry out the horrific deed and the job was done by a young Glasgow medical student.

Above: Broad Street and the Tolbooth.

Below: Opening Assizes – the Judges Parade, 1873.

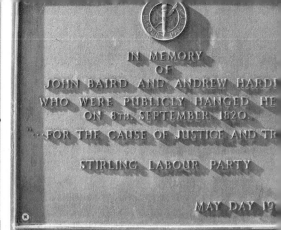

Above: The Tolbooth plaque.

Left: The Tolbooth.

The execution of Andrew Hardie and John Baird took place on Friday last, on a scaffold erected in front of the court-house, in Broad Street, in terms of their sentence, being convicted of high treason. About half past ten o' clock on Thursday night, workmen commenced to erect the scaffold, which was completed before morning. Two coffins, containing saw dust, one bearing the inscription, 'Andrew Hardie, aged 27', the other, 'John Baird, aged 37', were placed upon it; a board, covering about a third of the coffin, was placed to support the breast of the body; a square tub, in which was a considerable quantity of saw dust, was placed at the head of each coffin; to that side of the tub nearest the coffin was affixed a block. The shops in Broad Street and in the streets leading immediately into it were shut. A sight so appalling as the mangling of bodies by decapitation, prevented many persons from attending; they might be seen moving along other streets, under feelings corresponding to the melancholy event which was taking place on Broad Street. The bodies of Baird and Hardie, after hanging half an hour, were cut down and placed on their coffins, with the face downwards, the neck resting on the block, and head hanging into the tub. The headsman now came to perform his duty - he was a little man about 18 years of age, rather delicately made - he did not seem destined by nature for the office which he had undertaken, for he was exceedingly agitated. On his appearance a shudder pervaded the crowd, and cries of Murder! Murder! were raised. From his agitation, and consequent weakness, it required three strokes of the axe to sever the head of Hardie. He then held up the head with both hands, and, evidently with an effort, exclaimed - 'This is the head of a traitor'. Recovering some confidence, he decapitated Baird at two strokes. Having performed his duty, he hastily retired. He was observed to tremble greatly, and was heard to say, *I wish to God I had not it to do.*

The Stirling Journal, 8 April 1820

Granny Duncan, a local Stirling character, showed great kindness to Baird and Hardie when they were in Stirling Castle awaiting execution – smuggling letters and food into their cells. Both Baird and Hardie requested that Granny Duncan should attend after their executions. On the day of the executions, it is said that Hardie called out from the scaffold, 'Are you there, Granny?', to which she replied, 'Aye, Andrew, my puir laddie' – 'Bide to the end, then', were Hardie's last words to her.

The Tolbooth was adapted as a gallery and venue in 2001.

14. Town Clerk Norrie's House, Broad Street

The arrival of the railway at Stirling in 1848 was an incentive for development closer to the station and beyond the medieval burgh walls, which drew commercial activity away from the Top of the Town. By the early twentieth century Broad Street was in need of improvement with many of the buildings in a seriously dilapidated condition. From the 1930s, the area underwent extensive regeneration under the guidance of the architect Sir Frank Mears (1880–1953). Key historic buildings were restored and the reconstruction work was in a traditional Scots style.

James Norie, who seems to have had a good standing in his profession of notary, succeeded William Barclay as Town Clerk in 1650, and appears almost continuously to have retained his office down to 1679. He is shown by the Burgh Records to have been a discreet and efficient servant, and entrusted with many important commissions.

The Old Ludgings of Stirling, J. S. Fleming, 1871

Norrie's House is an original but much-restored seventeenth-century property marked with the inscription 1671. The frontage includes a number of inscribed religious and moral precepts: *IN SOLI DEO GLORIA A R* (Glory to God alone), *ARBOR VITAE SAPIENTIA* (Wisdom is the tree of life) and *MURUS AHENEUS BONA CONSCIENTIA* (A good conscience is a brazen wall). The inscribed initials IN and AR relate to Norrie and his wife, Agnes Robertson. Different sources give the initials AL and IR as Norrie's sister-in-law Jean Robertson and her husband or Agnes Robertson's parents.

The cannons in the view of Broad Street were made by Carron Iron Works. They were purchased by Stirling Council from the War Office in 1904.

Above left and right: Town Clerk Norrie's House.

15. Darnley's House, Bow Street

The High Street, or Broad Street, as it is now commonly called, is the principal street in Stirling. It lies, in the shape of a parallelogram, on the upper part of the hill whereon the town is built; and, what with the height of the houses, their substantial, and in various instances, antique architecture, the steeple of the town-house, and other favourable circumstances, it makes a very respectable appearance.

Picture of Stirling, Robert Chambers, 1830

Darnley House, at the foot of Broad Street, is said to have been the nursery of James VI and his son Prince Henry, but this is thought to be incorrect, as the Royal nursery was within the Castle. The property at one time belonged to the Erskines of Mar, who were hereditary keepers of the Castle, and also had charge of the heirs of the Scottish Throne from James V down to Prince Henry. It was afterwards sold by Thomas, Earl of Kellie, to Janet Kilbowie, who, between 1650 and 1660, conducted a successful tavern and a meeting place for municipal festivities. In the beginning of the last century the Bank of Scotland had offices on the first flat, and on their going down town, the Sherriff Clerk entered into possession of the premises, which were continued as his office until removal to the County Buildings.

The Old Ludgings of Stirling, J. S. Fleming, 1871

One of the few remaining historic houses fronting the foot of Broad Street has an inscribed stone reading 'Darnley House, the Nursery of James VI and of his son Prince Henry'. However, there is no evidence to support the statement. The house was the property of Alexander Erskine of Canglour, whose son Thomas, Earl of Kellie, sold it to Janet Kilbowie, who, between 1650 and 1660, ran it as a tavern which was a noted rendezvous of the magistrates and town council. In 1651, the Stirling authorities surrendered to Cromwell's General Monck in the tavern.

Above left and right: Darnley's House.

16. Stirling Boys' Club, St John Street

The Stirling Boys' Club opened in October 1929 with twenty-two members. It catered for boys who were not members of the Boys' Brigade or Scouts. Facilities included a large hall, which could be used as a games hall, gymnasium and concert hall; billiards; bagatelle; ping-pong and draughts. The club also organised competitive football, cricket, and boxing for the boys. The club was the inspiration of Major Frederick Maurice Crum (1872–1955). Major Crum's contribution as founder and principal benefactor of the club is commemorated on a plaque on the building.

Left: Stirling Boys' Club.

Below: Stirling Boys' Club detail.

The building is a reconstruction of the seventeenth-century Butter and Poultry Market at the corner of St John Street and Jail Wynd. The picturesque design by the artist and architect Eric Bell (1884–1973) includes a number of traditional Scottish architectural features: crow-stepped gables, moulded skewputts, stone-mullioned windows and dormers. The crest of the club, a St Andrew's Cross with a shield background and the year 1929 engraved below, is displayed above the doorway. Inspirational motto panels for the boys are inscribed on lintols: 'Play the Game', 'Keep Smiling' and 'Quarrelling is Taboo'.

17. Bruce of Auchenbowie's House, St John's Street

The house at the top of St John Street dates from the sixteenth century and is traditionally associated with Robert Bruce of Auchenbowie. The Bruce family were major landowners in Stirlingshire and Robert Bruce was Stirling's Provost in 1555. Although the building has been extensively altered and restored over the centuries, its prominent stair tower and traditional details still reflect its early origins.

Bruce of Auchenbowie's House.

18. Stirling Old Town Jail, St John Street

Stirling new prison, now finished, is situated near the top of St John Street, enclosed within a high wall, varying from fifteen to thirty-one feet in height. This prison, from its elevated situation, extent of building, and castellated appearance, presents a new feature in the picture of Stirling, and is seen with great advantage from various parts, but particularly from the river.

The Tourist's Companion Through Stirling, John Forbes, 1848

Opening of the New Jail - On Thursday last this great public house was opened for the accommodation of those of the lieges who have a penchant for a peculiar kind of treatment. The day was Martinmas, and althogh this time is merely a paying and not a flitting term in Stirling, yet, as our jail-birds work by the rule of contradictions, so our authorities, taking advantage of this trait in the habits of the jail poulation, resolved that as they do not pay rent they should at least flit upon the term-day. Accordingly, as early as five in the morning the movemenmt began, and in no very long period the old jail was evacuated, and the new one received the seventy-one prisoners then on hand, who are now as comfortable in their new habitation as the nature of the case will admit.

Stirling Observer, 18 November 1847

On 11 November 1847, the inmates from the prison block in the Tolbooth were marched to the new Stirling jail. The Tolbooth was described as the 'worst prison

Stirling Old Town Jail.

in Britain' and there may have been some relief for the prisoners in the new building with its ventilated individual cells, basic central heating system, washing facilities and rooftop exercise area.

The architect of the new County Jail was Thomas Brown (1806–72), the leading prison architect of the time, and he incorporated all the latest innovations in penal design. The regime was based on the separation of inmates – the solitude was intended to encourage repentance and avoid fraternisation – and the panopticon-like central domed guardhouse allowed warders to supervise every cell.

The foreboding fortress-like design of the building with its crenelated parapets, large round tower, gunloops and dark whinstone emphasised its menacing appearance and was a popular form for prison buildings at the time.

By the 1880s, prison accommodation was being centralised and, in 1888, the jail was taken over as a Military Detention Barracks. The army moved out in 1935 and the building was used by the local Civil Defence Volunteers during the Second World War. After the war, it was disused and derelict for a number of years. In 1996, it reopened as the Stirling Old Town Jail – a popular museum of incarceration with displays on the history of the building and the penal system in Scotland.

19. Former Erskine Church (Marykirk), St John Street

The foundation-stone of the building, known as Erskine United Presbyterian Church, was laid on 4th May, 1824, by Allan Johnstone, architect, Stirling. In a sealed bottle was placed a copy of the Stirling Journal, a medal struck upon His Majesty's coronation, one in commemoration of his visit to Scotland, specimens of the paper currency of the Stirling Bank, and a written paper with the following: The Reverend Ebenezer Erskine having been ejected from the West Church of Stirling in the year 1740, in consequence of a sentence of deposition pronounced by the General Assembly of the Church of Scotland, for his faithfulness in contending for the rights of the Christian people, those of the inhabitants of the town of Stirling and the neighbourhood, professing their adherence to those principles for the purity of which Mr Erskine testified, erected a place of worship for him in the same year a little in front of this spot.

Old Faces, Old Places and Old Stories of Stirling, William Drysdale, 1899

The Secession Church in St John Street was the first of that denomination in Scotland, and was founded by the Rev Ebenezer Erskine in 1738. The old building being found insufficient, the present handsome and commodious structure was erected in 1826, and can accommodate about 2000 sitters, who support respectably two clergyman. Mr Erskine is interred within the shrubbery in front of the church.

The Tourist's Companion Through Stirling, John Forbes, 1848

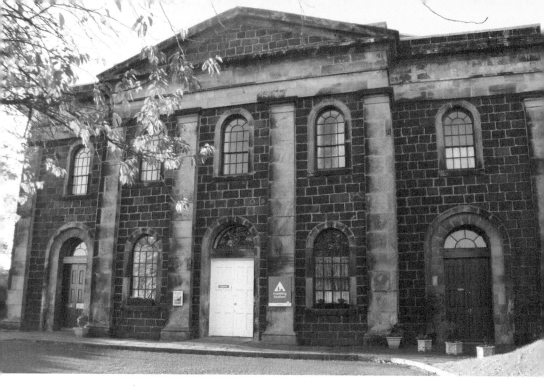

Above: The Erskine Church.

Left: Ebenezer Erskine Monument.

The classically fronted former Erskine Church, with its fine pedimented portico, dates from 1826. It was a replacement for an earlier church, dating from 1740, which was built for a Secession congregation led by Revd Ebenezer Erskine (1680–1754). In 1731, Erskine took up the ministry of the West Church in Stirling. However, his objections to certain doctrines of the established Church of Scotland resulted in his suspension from the ministry. This resulted in him founding a Secession church – the United Presbytery. Erskine was a popular preacher: 'Serious Christians from all quarters of the country, attracted by the celebrity of his character, were eager to enjoy occasionally the benefits of his ministry, and on sacramental occasions he had frequently attendants from the distance of sixty or seventy miles.'

The church was disused in 1968 and only the façade survived a fire in 1980. The new development behind the original façade is Stirling's youth hostel.

The imposing domed monument to Ebenezer Erskine dates from 1859, and was designed by Peddie & Kinnear. He was buried by his own wish, in the middle of his meeting house. It was erected over Erskine's original tomb in the earlier church.

2c. The Old High School, Spittal Street/Academy Road

The Old High School dates from 1856. The 1887–90 extension, by James Marjoribanks MacLaren, to the earlier school includes a tower with a revolving copper-domed observatory at the top of the building, which retains its original

The Old High School.

Above left: Old High School entrance door with signs of the zodiac.

Above right: Sir Henry Campbell-Bannerman statue.

Newtonian telescope. The observatory was gifted by Sir Henry Campbell-Bannerman. The school was converted into the Stirling Highland Hotel in 1990.

Sir Henry Cambell-Bannerman (1836–1908) was the Member of Parliament for the Stirling Burghs, which he represented for forty years, from 1868 until his death in 1908. He rose rapidly through the ranks of the Liberal Party, became leader in 1899 and was prime minister from 5 December 1905 until 3 April 1908. He has the honour of being the first person to have the official title prime minister (the former title of the position was First Lord of the Treasury). Campbell-Bannerman's government introduced a number of social reforms based on his liberal beliefs. He resigned as prime minister on 3 April 1908 due to ill health following a series of heart attacks, and was replaced by Henry Asquith. Campbell-Bannerman continued to live at No. 10 Downing Street due to his worsening health. He passed away on 22 April 1908 and is the only former prime minister to die within the building.

Cambell-Bannerman is commemorated by a statue on Corn Exchange Road. The statue of Campbell-Bannerman by Paul Montford was unveiled on 1 November 1913 by Prime Minister Herbert Asquith. Asquith, who opposed votes for women, was attacked by suffragettes at Bannockburn on his way to the unveiling ceremony.

21. Former Spittal's Hospital, Spittal Street

Following Stirling's years of abject poverty, while its paupers became an intolerable annoyance to the surrounding districts, hospitals for the relief of decayed tradesmen or burgesses were built, until the town was veritably a colony of asylums. Spittal's, although not the most important, is the oldest of the number. A house in the Back Row has the following inscription, with the scissors en saltier: - *This hovs is foundit for svpport of the pvir be Robert Spittal, tailyovr to King Jaemes the 4, in anno, 1530. - R.S.*

The History of Stirlingshire, William Nimmo, 1880

This is an endowment which was left by Robert Spittal, tailor to James IV, for the support of decayed members of the seven incorporated trades. The amount of the sum or the exact time of its bequeathment, and even the direct object intended by the donor are not known; only there is reason to believe that it was the design of Spittal that the objects of his charity should reside together and wear a particular dress. From this the hospital seems to have been originally intended for an alms house, but as this is a mode of receiving charity alien to the feelings of the Scottish people, the original intention has been changed, and the poor receive a weekly allowance at their own houses. This sum is greatly less than it was some years ago, owing to a very injudicious purchase of landed property, and also owing to there having been too many pensioners receiving charity. The weekly allowance amounts to from Is. to Is. 9d per week. This is the more to be regretted as the number of poor people entitled to receive assistance is very great; but this cannot be helped, for if the council would ever wish to retrieve the affairs of the charity, the funds must be husbanded. The annual income of the hospital amounts to about £700. In its present reduced state it costs the town council very little trouble, almost every fresh application being rejected whenever it is mentioned.

A New Description of the Town and Castle of Stirling, 1835

Robert Spittal made his fortune as tailor to King James IV (1473–1513). He was a significant philanthropist, providing funds to assist the poor in Stirling and to 'build bridges in the neighbourhood' (the Old Bridge at Bannockburn and the Bridge of Teith). In 1530, Spittal's Hospital was opened in the Nether Hospital on Irvine Place. The current building with its crow-stepped gable, conical-roofed round stair tower, and slate roof dates from around 1650. The inscribed panel on the frontage of the Spittal Street building includes a set of tailor's scissors to acknowledge Spittal's trade and was moved to its present location from the Irvine Place building. The building was restored and divided into tenement flats in 1959 by Robert Naismith (1916–2004).

The adjoining building, Glengarry Lodge or the Darrow Lodging, is another important seventeenth-century building from Stirling's historic past. It was the town house of lawyer Sir James Darrow in 1521 and was also restored in 1959.

Above: Spittal's Hospital and the Darrow Lodging.

Left: Spittal's Hospital plaque.

22. No. 53 Baker Street and No. 1 Bank Street

Baker Street was previously called Baxter's Wynd. It runs uphill between King Street and Bow Street and was the main road through Stirling, prior to the development of Murray Place in 1842. The street was the subject of a substantial amount of sensitive reconstruction from the 1930s in a sympathetic traditional vernacular style by architect Sir Frank Mears (1880–1953), who was planning consultant to the burgh.

Baker Street/Bank Street building.

Baker Street/Bank Street
building plaque.

    Amidst all this traditional stone-built architecture, the Old English-style building on the corner of Baker Street and Bank Street, with its half-timbered gable, oriel window, and banded polychromatic brickwork, is particularly distinctive. It dates from 1890 and was designed by John Allan (1847–1922). The plaque on the frontage with the Stirling coat of arms (*Sterlini Opidum*) is a characteristic feature of John Allan's buildings in Stirling.

23. John Cowane's House, St Mary's Wynd

John Cowane was one of Stirling's wealthiest and most influential merchants – shipowner, wine merchant, banker, town councillor, Member of Parliament for Stirling and Dean of the Merchant Guild. His house on St Mary's Wynd, which dates from 1603, was one of the largest in the town.

    Cowane never married and lived at the house with his sister, Agnes – although in 1611 he was fined for fathering a child out of wedlock. The building was purchased by Cowane's Hospital in 1924 and is now preserved as a picturesque ruin.

    On his death in 1633, Cowane left large sums of money to numerous charitable causes in Stirling.

Above and right: John
Cowane's House.

24. Atheneum, King Street

The Atheneum is another public building, forming an ornament to the top of King Street. On the ground floor are shops; the flats above are occupied as a reading-room and subscription library. The library contains many thousand works of sterling merit, and of the first literary compositions of the day.

The Tourist's Companion Through Stirling, John Forbes, 1848

The building with the Gothic spire at the head of King Street opened on 17 January 1818. The first floor was occupied by the Stirling Subscription Reading Room and the upper floor by the Stirling Library. The ground-floor shops were initially occupied by Patrick Connal, a merchant; Miss Fletcher, a haberdasher; and Drummond & Sons, seedsmen. A & J Moffat, drapers, were later long-time occupiers of the shops.

The building was known rather grandly as the Atheneum, from the Latin for a place of learning – it is more widely known locally as the Steeple. It was on the site of the Mealmarket, the demolition of which divided the town council. The building was converted to council offices in 1873.

The statue on the Atheneum is known as the Wee Wallace to distinguish it from the larger statue of Wallace by David Watson Stevenson on the National Wallace Monument. It portrays Wallace in classical garb with a sword on his back and holding a horn. It was sculpted by Handyside Ritchie for William Drummond and was originally situated in Drummond's own garden. In 1859, it was presented to the town – a new porch was added to the building with the statue on top. The motto '*Nemo me impune laccesit*' (No one shall attack me with impunity) inscribed on the porch is the motto of Scotland.

King Street.

Above left and right: Atheneum.

Right: Wee Wallace.

25. The Golden Lion Hotel, Nos 8–10 King Street

King Street was part of the old Hie Gait or High Street of Stirling. In 1820, the name Quality Street was changed to King Street on the Coronation of King George IV. The location of the New Port, one of the burgh gates, is marked on the roadway outside the Golden Lion Hotel.

The Golden Lion Hotel first opened its doors to visitors in 1786 as Wingate's Inn, after James Wingate, a local businessman who had commissioned the new hotel – the architect was Gideon Gray. It stood on the site of the Gibb's Inn Tavern, an earlier coaching inn. In 1897, it was advertised as 'the largest and finest Hotel in Stirling providing every home comfort, combined with moderate charges'.

On 26 August 1787, Robert Burns visited Stirling Castle on his Highland tour and stayed at Wingate's. At the time the castle was in a dilapidated condition and this encouraged Burns to use a diamond pen to scratch the famous 'Stirling Lines' on a pane of glass in his bedroom:

The Golden Lion Hotel.

Here Stewarts once in glory reign'd,
And laws for Scotland's weal ordain'd;
But now unroof'd their palace stands,
Their sceptre fallen to other hands:
Fallen indeed, and to the earth,
Whence grovelling reptiles take their birth!
The injured Stewart line is gone;
A race outlandish fills their throne:
An idiot race, to honour lost -
Who know them best despise them most.

On a return visit in October 1787, realising that the poem had caused offence and its pro-Jacobite sentiment was potentially treasonable, Burns smashed the pane of glass.

The lines were inscribed in stone at the entrance to the Stirling Smith Museum on 12 March 2002, the day that Stirling became a city.

26. Former Drummond Tract Building, King Street/Murray Place

The fine building at the corner of Murray Place and King Street is now occupied by the British Linen Company Bank, but was built for the Stirling Tract Enterprise, originated by the late Peter Drummond. This explains the sculptured heads of Reformers and Divines with which the building is profusely adorned, and which do not seem altogether appropriate to the business of a banking company. The Tract Enterprise so grew in dimensions that even this large building was found too small for its requirements, and a new and larger depot was some years ago erected in Dumbarton Road off Port Street.

Guide to Stirling in 1911

The striking and ornately detailed building with its barley twist columns at the corner of Murray Place and King Street was built as the new headquarters of Peter Drummond's Tract Enterprise in 1862. The building was originally decorated with two angelic figures in the corner niche of the upper floor and the busts of John Knox, Marin Luther and other religious figures.

Mr. Peter Drummond was not only a good man, but he had the courage of his convictions. He was not what the Bishop of Liverpool calls a jellyfish Christian. It is said that he unconsciously originated the Stirling Tract Enterprise by publishing a tract on Sabbath desecration. This was in the month of August, 1848, the year when the Scottish Central Railway was opened from Greenhill to Perth. Ten thousand copies of this tract were printed and distributed among the

Sabbath breakers in Cambuskenneth gardens and elsewhere, and within three months one hundred thousand copies were in demand. So gratifying were the results that Mr. Drummond resolved to continue the good work.

The Merchants' Guide to Stirling, 1897

Peter Drummond (1799–1877), a Stirling seed merchant, was a particularly devout individual. In 1848, he published a religious tract railing against what he considered to be the blasphemous operation of the Cambuskenneth Ferry on the Sabbath.

The ferry boat connection between Stirling and Cambuskenneth dated back for centuries. The ferry avoided the much longer journey by way of Causewayhead and Stirling Bridge. The Patrons of Cowane's Hospital ran the ferry between 1709 and 1935. The ferry was much in demand during the Berry Fair, when Stirling residents would make the crossing to buy the produce. Proposals to replace the Cambuskenneth Ferry with a bridge were discussed from the early part of the nineteenth century and rumbled on into the early twentieth century. In 1930, Cowane's Hospital gave notice of the intention to discontinue the ferry service, since it was not obliged to supply one, and derived no profit from it. There were

Below left and right: Former Drummond Tract Building.

also complaints that the ferry was unsafe and inconvenient. This spurred on the authorities and the opening of the new footbridge on 23 October 1935 marked the end of the ferry.

Hundreds of thousands of copies of Drummond's tract were distributed and this led to him establishing the Stirling Tract Enterprise, which expanded to become the foremost nineteenth-century publisher of religious pamphlets.

The building was used as a branch of the British Linen Bank from 1887, when the increase in the Tract Enterprise's business made a move to larger premises on Dumbarton Road necessary. The Tract Enterprise closed for business in 1980.

27. Thistles Shopping Centre

Stirling has always been the main market town for the county with a full range of retail outlets. The opening of the massive Thistles Shopping Centre, in 1977, in the centre of the town, cemented Stirling's position as an important regional shopping destination.

Murray Place before redevelopment.

Murray Place after redevelopment.

Murray Place was originally a narrow lane leading to orchards around the site of the railway station. It was developed in 1842 to connect King Street to the new bridge over the Forth and to reduce traffic through the upper part of the town. It was named for William Murray of Touchadam & Polmaise (1773–1847), who was the Lieutenant Colonel of the Stirlingshire Yeomanry in 1843 and influential in the formation of the new street. Murray Place became commercially more important when the railway arrived in 1848.

The development of the Thistles Centre, and adjacent retail outlets, resulted in significant alterations to the area. These included the demolition of the Norman-style North Parish Church, with its low and massive square tower, which dated from 1843, and the removal of the Gothic-fronted Baptist Chapel of 1854. The Thistles Centre also resulted in the loss of Orchard Place, which ran parallel to the east of Murray Place.

A preserved circular guardroom in a bastion of the town wall is a unique feature of the Thistles Centre. It is accessed down a flight of spiral stairs from the main mall area. It originally protected an angle of the Burgh Wall and includes a sunken 'Thieves Pot' or 'Bottle Dungeon'. Two replica Stirling Heads representing Apollo and a king, possibly James V, are displayed in the bastion.

Above: The Thistles Centre entrance.

Right: The entrance to the Thistles Bastion.

28. The Stirling Arcade

Next Friday Mr W Crawford will open his hall in the Arcade Buildings with a grand concert by London artists, and we have no doubt that the public will give the pushing proprietor a good house. On the Friday following Mr Crawford's friends will entertain him to dinner to celebrate the completion of the Stirling Arcade. Provost Anderson is to preside.

Alloa Advertiser, 9 September 1882

The Stirling Arcade.

The Stirling Arcade.

The Stirling Arcade (also known as the Alhambra Arcade and Crawford Arcade) is one of only five shopping arcades in Scotland – the others are the Central Arcade, Ayr (1880); the North Bridge Arcade, Edinburgh (1900); the Argyle Arcade, Glasgow (1827); and the Market Arcade, Inverness (1860).

The arcade was the brainchild of William Crawford, a Stirling china merchant and town councillor, and it opened in 1882. The architect was John McLean. Crawford's idea was to link Murray Place to King Street – an astute business move, as he owned shops on both streets.

The arcade originally included thirty-nine shops and was fronted at both ends by two hotels with grand facades: the Douglas in Murray Place and the Temperance in King Street. The Arcade Theatre was situated within the arcade above the shops and was accessed by a stairway. It seated up to 1,200 and, following a number of short leases, was taken over by William Crawford in 1912. It was renamed the Alhambra Music Hall and hosted many well-known variety performers during its heyday. It was converted to a cinema in 1930, closed in 1939 and was converted to a shop in 1964.

The recent restoration and redecoration of the arcade has created a unique up-to-date shopping setting within this rare historic asset.

29. Stirling Railway Station, Goosecroft Road

Stirling was a historic port which supported overseas trade and had a daily steamer service to and from Leith. The railway, which first came to Stirling in 1848, started the decline of the river trade and by the mid-twentieth century the port had ceased to operate.

The present railway station building in Stirling, with its picturesque battlements and crow stepped gables, opened in 1916 following a major rebuild by the Caledonian Railway Company. It is one of the finest station buildings in Scotland and was designed by the architect James Miller, who is notable for the quality of his Scottish railway stations. The railway made commuting easier and resulted in a substantial expansion of the town.

The road leading down to the station from Murray Place cuts through what was in ancient times the burying-ground of the Dominican Friars.

Above and below: Stirling railway station.

3c. The Engine Shed, Forthside Way

The Engine Shed is Historic Environment Scotland's national building conservation centre. It was opened in July 2017 by Fiona Hyslop, Cabinet Secretary for Culture, Tourism and External Affairs.

The Engine Shed building was built around 1890 as part of the strategically important Forthside military base. The site was sold in the 1990s and most of the infrastructure associated with the Engine Shed was removed.

From 2013, the original building was transformed to create the new conservation centre. The existing building was sympathetically refurbished with the addition of two new zinc and glass extensions. The scale and form of the extensions were carefully designed to reflect the character of the original building. The completed building is a striking landmark which exemplifies the best in the conservation and reuse of historic structures.

The Engine Shed is now the base for Historic Environment Scotland's nationally important building conservation research and education facility. The aim is to inspire interest in Scotland's built heritage by interactive displays and other events.

The development has won a number of awards since its opening, including recognition as one of the best new buildings in Scotland by the Royal Incorporation of Architects in Scotland.

The Engine Shed.

31. The Wolfcraig Building and the Stirling Wolf, Port Street/
     Dumbarton Road

Then there is the Wolf Crag in Port Street, of which we have the following
legend. During the reign of Donald V, near the close of the ninth century, two
Northumbrian princes, named Osbrecht and Ella, had acquired by conquest
all south of the Forth from Stirling, and toward the eastern coast. The town
was under the rule of these Anglo-Saxons for some twenty-eight years. About
the same period the Danes, under their magical flag, the Black Raven, had
visited Britain for pillage. Pursuing their depredations to the north, each town
inhabited by Anglo-Saxons was as well guarded and watched as could be for
the approach of these invaders. At the South Port of Stirling, a sentinel had been
set; but, overcome with fatigue, he fell asleep on duty, and was awakened by
the growl of a wolf which had left the woody wilds for a rock in the immediate
neighbourhood. Getting roused in time to see some of the northern hordes on the
advance, he at once alarmed the garrison, who speedily caused a retreat.

The History of Stirlingshire, William Nimmo, 1880

Port Street takes its name from the Barras Yett, the main burgh gate, which was
the principal entrance to Stirling from the south in the days of the town wall. It
was located at the junction of Port Street and Dumbarton Road and is marked by
a brass plaque on the pavement. The historic route through the town passed into
King Street before ascending Spittal Street and Bow Street to the bottom of Broad
Street. It then descended by St Mary's Wynd towards Stirling Old Bridge. The
demolition of the Barras Yett in 1770 allowed the development of new streets –
Port Street, Murray Place and Barnton Street – at the edge of the old burgh.

The ornate red-brick Wolfcraig Building dates from 1897 to 1898 and
was built in Welsh red brick as a high-class grocer's shop for Macfarlane
and Robertson to a design by John Allan (1847–1922). It was one of the first
buildings in the country to be built with a steel frame and is embellished with a
sculpture of a wolf and the inscription:

Here in auld days
The Wolf roam'd
In a hole in the rock
In ambush lay.

The building celebrates the legend dating from the ninth century that Stirling
was saved from a Viking invasion when a howling wolf provided an alert of the
imminent attack in time for the defence of the town. Since then, like Rome, the
wolf has been adopted as the town's emblem, appearing on the coat of arms, burgh
seals and buildings throughout the town. There is a degree of irony in this, as the
last wolf in Scotland is reputed to have been killed near Stirling in the 1740s.

Above: The Wolfcraig
Building.

Right: The Wolfcraig
Building plaque.

Here in auld days
The wolf roam'd
In a hole of the rock
In ambush lay

32. The Black Boy Fountain, Allan Park

The distinctive Black Boy Fountain is located in Allan Park, a small green area at the junction of King's Park Road and St Ninians Road, which was Stirling's seventeenth-century site of public execution and burial, 'the Gallous Mailing'.

> In the year 1350, there was, in the kingdom of Scotland, so great a pestilence and plague among men (which also prevailed for a great many years before and after, in divers parts of the world - nay, all over the whole earth), as, from the beginning of the world even unto modern times, had never been heard of by man, nor is found in books, for the enlightenment of those who come after. For, to such a pitch did that plague wreck its cruel spite that nearly a third of mankind were thereby made to pay the debt of Nature. Moreover, by God's will, this evil led to a strange and unwonted kind of death, insomuch that the flesh of the sick was somehow puffed out and swollen, and they dragged out their earthly life for barely two days. Men shrank from it so much that, through fear of contagion, sons, fleeing as from the face of leprosy or from an adder, durst not go and see their parents in the throes of death.

Gesta Annalia, John of Fordun, 1363

The fountain was erected in 1849 to commemorate the epidemic of bubonic plague in Stirling in 1369 which, in the cramped conditions within the town walls, killed a third of the population. The 1369 epidemic was one of a series of

Below left and right: The Black Boy Fountain.

The Black Boy Fountain and the Christie Memorial Clock.

outbreaks of the Great Mortality in the fourteenth century, which was repeated in the seventeenth century.

> The Black Boy Fountain was one of the exclusive attractions of Stirling some years ago, when it was floodlit with vari-coloured electric lanterns - a feature that should be revived when peace is restored.

> *The Stirling Observer*, 2 November 1942

Over the years the fountain was central to events in Stirling. It was the rendezvous point for scouts and troops, and for the town's lavish VE Day celebrations on 8 May 1945, crowds gathered to see it illuminated with fairy lights and appreciate 'the amplified recorded music played from a Messrs Burgess and Speedie van'.

In 1943, a correspondent to the *Stirling Observer* recalled a time in the 'Black Boy's life when he misbehaved himself so much that the *unco guid* raised a hue and cry over his misconduct'. It seems that a 'local wag, out on a Saturday night frolic slipped a nice little sark over his nakedness'. It was recalled as a 'time when people did not live at such break-neck speed, and such a trifling episode caused no end of good-natured chaff for days'.

The fountain was manufactured by the Neilson Foundry of Glasgow and was restored in 1997 by the Ballantine Ironworks of Bo'ness as part of a regeneration project for Stirling town centre. It seems that at some point the Black Boy was made more respectable for public display by the removal of part of his anatomy.

The adjoining Christie Memorial Clock was unveiled in 1906. George Christie (1826–1904) was a well-known businessman in Stirling who was Provost between 1870 and 1879. In 1905, there were reports of human skulls being uncovered during the excavations for the installation of the clock. The presence of the human remains was accounted for by the fact that the ground was formerly the place of public execution where miscreants were hanged and buried on the spot.

33. Stirling Town Wall

Despite Stirling's naturally defensive site, an immense Town Wall was constructed from 1547 during the time of conflict, between 1543 and 1551, when King Henry VIII of England was attempting to force an alliance between England and Scotland by the marriage of his son, Edward, to the young Mary, Queen of Scots. A period later referred to by Sir Walter Scott as the 'Rough Wooing'. The wall originally ran from the castle to the Barras Yett and onwards to the bastion

Stirling town wall.

Above and below: Stirling town wall.

preserved in the Thistles Shopping Centre. The remaining sections of the wall in Stirling are the most complete example of this type of defence in Scotland.

The Back Walk is a 'fine wooded public airing ground' and follows the historic city walls providing stunning panoramic vistas of the surrounding area. The walk was constructed under the patronage of William Edmonstone, the Laird of Cambuswallace. It was originally built in 1724 from the rear of the former High School to Lady Hill, and was extended in the 1790s to Dumbarton Road and around the castle to the Gowanhill. It is the oldest publicly maintained road in Scotland.

34. Allan Park South Church

Yesterday the Allan Park Church, Stirling, under the pastorate of the Rev. Mr. Gowanlock, was opened for public worship. This new church has been erected by a party who seceded from the Erskine UP Church in consequence of a dispute relating to certain matters of fact in connection with the membership. The church is situated to the east end of the town, between the Back Walk and the Dumbarton Road, the entrance being from the Back Walk. The central gable of the church is flanked by a large square tower on the one side, and on the other by a one storey builidng. The door of the church, which is in the centre of the gable, is richly moulded, and has columns with carved capitals supporting a moulded arch, over which is a drip stone. The tower, which flanks the principal front of the church at Dumbarton Road, is perfectly square. The church is in the early Gothic style of architecture, with more of the Scottish character than is generally given in modern buildings. The interior of the church is plainly, though most substantially, finished and fitted up, roomy and comfortable accommodation being the principal object in view. The church is seated for rather more than 700 persons. The whole church has been got up at an expense of about £4,500, being somewhat more than the contract price. Yesterday, special opening services were held. The church was filled with a large audience, including a great number of the gentry of the town and county. The Rev. Dr. King, of London, preached in the forenoon and took occasion to refer to the circumstaces in which the congregation were now placed, and congratulated them on the very beautiful erection in which they were now assembled for divine worship. The Rev. Mr Gowanlock officiated in the afternoon, and preached an appropriate discourse. The collection from the two diets amounted in all to about £230.

Glasgow Daily Herald, 21 October 1867

The elegant Allan Park Church stands on a steep-sloping site on the north side of Albert Place. The church was designed by the eminent architectural practice of John Dick Peddie (1824–91) and Charles George Hood Kinnear (1830–94).

Allan Park South Church.

Allan Park South Church.

35. Statue of Robert Burns, Corn Exchange Road

Robert Burns (1759–96), the National Bard of Scotland, is depicted in more statues around the world than any other literary figure. Stirling's bronze statue of Burns by Albert H. Hodge was gifted by Provost Bayne and was unveiled on 23

Statue of Robert Burns.

September 1914 by his daughter. During a visit to Stirling in August 1787, Burns wrote 'just now, from Stirling Castle, I have seen by the setting sun the glorious prospect of the windings of Forth through the rich carse of Stirling'.

36. Stirling War Memorial, Corn Exchange Road

The Stirling War Memorial was designed by Stirling architect George R. Davidson and was unveiled on 14 October 1922 by Field Marshal Earl Haig. It consists of a square column in a walled enclosure topped by a flagpole with bronze wreaths on each side and two lions holding a crown. The inscription reads: 'In Proud And Grateful Memory Of The Men Of Stirling Who Gave Their Lives In The World War/ At The Going Down Of The Sun And In The Morning We Will Remember Them/ This Memorial Was Unveiled By Field Marshall Earl Haig/14th October 1922.' It is a fittingly prominent memorial to the 711 men of Stirling who gave their lives in the First World War and the 211 in the Second World War. The memorial was restored in 2014.

Stirling War Memorial.

Stirling War Memorial.

37. Stirling Library

The building contains on the ground floor a large, well-lighted entrance hall and lending library, having an open timbered roof and large top lights. The news and reading-room occupies the whole of the frontage to the back, a very handsome room. Convenient to the entrance are the newspaper stands for sixteen newspapers, and seating accommodation for eight-four readers at the tables. The juvenile room has accommodation for twenty-four readers. The upper floor is occupied by the reference library arranged to hold eight thousand volumes, seating accommodation is provided for forty readers - a section of this room is for lady readers. The librarian's house is entirely detached from the other parts of the building. The exterior is designed in a late phase of Scottish architecture, and as the site widens out towards the lower end the building is brought out in a series of breaks. The building is partly built of whinstone rock quarried from the site.

Edinburgh Evening News, 8 February 1904

The Stirling Public Library was formally opened on 6 February 1904 in front of a 'large and representative assemblage'. Andrew Carnegie had donated £7,000 to fully meet the costs and the memorial stone for the building had been laid by

Stirling Library.

Mrs Carnegie on 11 October 1902. Carnegie had noted that 'after comparing all the uses to which surplus wealth could be put, I have been led to the conclusion that the greatest and best use of all is to devote to the building of free public libraries for communities which evince a willingness to maintain them'. Carnegie had requested that the building should be designed in the Scottish style with decorative architectural treatment appropriate to a public building in the historic town of Stirling. The bold, graceful design of the new library on its commanding site more than met his expectations and he was said to have noted that he had never seen such a handsome building erected for the money. The library was 'fitted with all the latest improvements', to a design by Mr Ramsay Henry Taylor, and could hold 20,000 volumes.

The library was formally handed over to Provost Thomson, who declared it open and expressed his gratitude to Dr Carnegie for his munificence. Provost Thomson hoped that the library would be a source of pride, comfort and enjoyment to the people of Stirling for generations to come. The guests were then shown around the library and tea was served in several rooms.

38. Stirling Municipal Buildings

Saturday last was a memorable day in Stirling, the two great events being the visit of the King and Queen, and the laying of the foundation stone of the new municipal buildings presently being erected on Corn Exchange Road. The stone was laid by His Majesty pressing an electric button at the County Buildings, and the current set in motion the machinery that lowered the stone into its place. Previous to the arrival of the King, however, there was a formal ceremony at the new buildings, when a number of articles (bound volumes of charters and other documents relating to the burgh, local and national newspapers, a jar containing coins of the realm and photographs of members of the Town Council) were enclosed in a leaden casket and placed in a cavity in the stone. In connection with the electrical apparatus used by the King in laying the foundation stone, it is of interest to note that the handle of the switch which closed the circuit was made from a piece of oak taken from the West Church of Stirling, and it is supposed to be about 600 years old. The design of the handle harmonises with that of the

Stirling Municipal Buildings.

Stirling
Municipal
Buildings
entrance.

building, which are to be in a French Renaissance style. A chaste silver band round the centre, embodying the details of the old burgh seal of Stirling, was the work of the Scottish Guild of Handicrafts, Stirling.

The Stirling Observer, 14 July 1914

Stirling's Municipal Buildings are a fine example of Edwardian civic building design which reflects the burgh's historic importance. The design was the result of a competition, won by John Gaff Gillespie (1870–1926) in 1908.

Above *left*: Laying the foundation stone at the Municipal Buildings.

Above right: Workmen and boys on the Municipal Buildings.

The foundation stone was laid on Saturday 11 July 1914 by King George V. However, because of unrest in the town due to the expenditure on the building at a time when many people were living in slum housing, this had to be done by remote control with the king safely ensconced at the County Buildings in Viewforth. Due to the First World War, work was delayed and the building did not open for business until 1918.

39. Albert Halls

The Albert Halls are Stirling's main venue main for concerts and other events. They opened on 5 October 1883 with a performance of the Messiah by the local choral society. The need for a proper hall in Stirling had been a long-standing issue in the town as 'the Corporation were too much hampered to carry out anything like an adequate scheme'. The choral society had resorted to fitting out the Smith Institute for their annual concerts. Matters were 'brought to a crisis' by the search for an assembly room by the promoters of the Stirling county ball and the requirement for a suitable hall for training of the Highland Borderers Militia. Mr R. Smith of Brentham Park, president of the choral society, took the lead in the formation of a Public Hall Company. £6,000 was subscribed to the company in a few weeks, the City Guildry Incorporation subscribed £1,000 and further donations were made by 'Sons of the Rock' at home and abroad. Plans were prepared by local architect William Simpson and work got underway in May 1881.

The building is classic in design, and has a massive and imposing appearance. In front is a large open space which has been laid out as ornamental ground.

Albert Halls.

The building contains two halls, a large hall and a lesser one, which have independent entrances and can be used simultaneously without in any way interfering with the proceedings in either. The large hall is seated for about 1300, and the small one for about 300. Both are well lighted, and the floors have been laid with polished pine for dancing. The hall, having corridors on three sides, will be free from draughts, and no effort has been spared to make it comfortable as well as safe. The front seats in the large hall are cushioned in rose-coloured Utrecht velvet. Cloak-room accommodation, an important accessory to public halls, has been amply provided. The building is admirably suited for public banquets or soirees. The large hall is adapted for a theatre in the most complete style, Mr Knapp, of the Theatre Royal, Glasgow, having been entrusted with the equipment. The back of the platform has been specially constructed for the reception of the organ now being built by Mr Willis, of London.

Glasgow Herald, 28 September 1883

4C. Glebe Crescent

Every road which leads out of the town, is now lined with neat modern villas which speak towards the wealth and comfort of the inhabitants; many of these are occupied by persons of fortune or annuitants, who have retired, after an adventurous life, to spend the conclusion of their days in their native town.

Picture of Stirling, Robert Chambers, 1830

Above and below: Glebe Crescent.

Stirling has utterly got quit of its ragged notoriety. It is, in fact, rapidly taking rank as one of the fashionable places of resort; and many of the villas on the outskirts of the burgh are little short of princely in their elegance of architecture.

The History of Stirlingshire, William Nimmo, 1880

In the nineteenth century, there was a significant development of pleasant suburban villas around Stirling. Glebe Crescent is a good example of these substantial mid- to late Victorian stone villas. The ornamental iron railings at the front of the houses in the earlier image would have been removed for the war effort in the 1940s. Railings and gates were removed throughout the country during the Second World War following a direction by Lord Beaverbrook, the wartime Minister of Supply. There is some debate about what happened to them after they were removed. It is claimed that the metal was unsuitable for reprocessing and that they were dumped at sea. There are stories that there was so much offloaded in parts of the Thames that the vast quantity of iron disrupted ships' compasses. It is also claimed that they were used as ballast in ships – with many houses in African seaports being festooned with fine Georgian railings salvaged in the destination ports. The removal of so much ornamental cast iron was a great architectural loss. However, even if they never became guns and tanks it was seen as a morale-boosting exercise.

41. Stirling Smith Art Gallery and Museum

The inhabitants of the ancient burgh of Stirling held holiday yesterday in honour of the opening of the Smith Institute, an event which had been anticipated for months past with a growing degree of interest. This valuable institution, which combines in itself a fine art gallery, a museum, and a public library, has been erected and endowed from funds amounting to the sum of £22,000, bequeathed for the purpose by the late Mr Thomas Stewart Smith of, Fitzroy Square, London, and formerly of Glassingall, in the county of Perth. An artist by profession, Mr Smith's chief design in making the bequest was to cultivate among the people a love of the fine arts; and the later years of his life were devoted to gathering together the nucleus of the collection which now adorns the walls of the Institute. The building which is in the Italian style of architecture, is from designs prepared by David Lessels, architect, Edinburgh, and, in addition to the merit of a pleasing exterior, possesses the important requisite of being admirably adapted for the uses to which it is applied. The inaugural ceremony took place in the picture gallery of the Institute. The weather, unfortunately, proved most unfavourable. Rain fell heavily during the whole forenoon and it was impossible to move about the streets with any degree of comfort and pleasure; but not withstanding there was a large attendance of the townspeople and of the residents of the surrounding district.

The Glasgow Herald, 12 August 1874

The Smith Institute was formally opened by Sir William Stirling Maxwell, MP, on 11 August 1874. The day was declared an official holiday in Stirling and it was an event for celebration in the town, with shops closing early to allow people to attend the opening.

Above and below: Stirling Smith Art Gallery.

The neat little neoclassical building with its Roman Doric portico was funded by a bequest of £22,000 from Thomas Stuart Smith of Glassingall, Perthshire. Smith, who was a talented artist and an affluent art collector, donated his own paintings and art collection to the Institute.

The Institute originally contained a picture gallery, museum and a reading room. It is now known as the Stirling Smith Art Gallery and Museum, and is a significant cultural and community asset for Stirling.

The gallery houses an excellent collection of Scottish artwork and some unique artefacts, including the world's oldest football and the Stirling Jug, which dates from 1457 and was used as the standard for Scottish measures.

Under the keeping of the governor of the old prison are a few ancient curiosities, particularly the Pint Measure, but better known by the name of the Stirling Jug, appointed to be the legal standard for dry and liquid measure, by an act of the

Scottish Parliament in 1437. It is made of a sort of coarse brass, and weighs 14 lb. 12 oz. 2 dr. Scottish Troy. Its mean depth is 6 inches; its diameter at the top 4.17 inches, and at the bottom 5.25 inches. It contains 103.404 cubic inches, or 3 lb. 7 oz. Scots Troy weight, of clear river water, being equal to 3 lb. 11 oz. 13.44 dr. Avoirdupois. The handle of the Jug is fastened to it with two brass nails, and the whole has an appearance of antiquity and rudeness quite characteristic of its very early age.

A New Description of the Town and Castle of Stirling, 1835

42. The Beheading Stone, Mote Hill

The beheading stone on Mote Hill was used for capital punishments in the fifteenth century. It is circular with a number of holes to hold the wooden beheading block. Heiding Hill, the alternative name for Mote Hill, alludes to the grisly use of the site. The stone was used in the execution of some notable people including the Duke of Albany, his second son, Alexander, and his father-in-law, the Earl of Lennox, in 1424. Sir Robert Graham and some of his associates in the assassination of King James I were also executed in 1437 on Heiding Hill. The stone is now on a concrete base and is protected by an iron grille, but the axe marks from executions are still visible.

The Beheading Stone.

The homely name of Hurly-hawky, bestowed on the spot upon which we now stand, is supposed to be derived from the circumstance, that, in ancient times, children were in the habit of amusing themselves in sliding down the inclined plane, formed by the slope of the hill, sitting upon the skeleton of a cow's head; hawky being, in Scotland, a common name for a cow. This circumstance is a proof, among many others, of the low state of mechanical invention in Scotland, in old times, when even the wealthy classes, were under the necessity of employing so uncouth a play-thing for their amusement, as the skeleton of a cow's head.

A New Description of the Town and Castle of Stirling, 1835

The Mote Hill was traditionally known locally as Hurly-hawky, derived from a local pastime which involved sliding down the hill on a cow's head skeleton. The two cannons on the hill were purchased by the town council from the army at Stirling Castle and moved to the hill for decorative purposes.

43. Stirling Old and New Bridges

The old bridge is by far the most noted structure of the kind in Scotland. It is the first erection of the sort which occurs on the Forth; and was, till lately, almost the only access for wheeled carriages from the south into the north of Scotland. Its age is unknown. The first mention made of it is in 1571, when Archbishop Hamilton was hanged on it by the king's faction, under the regent Lennox. General Blackeney, the governor of the castle, caused the south arch to be destroyed in 1745, in order to intercept the Highlanders.

The Tourist's Companion Through Stirling, John Forbes, 1848

The Old Bridge, an ancient relic, much admired for its spacious and lofty arches; venerable from its antiquity; beautiful from its situation; and interesting in the highest degree on account of its celebrity in Scottish history.

A New Description of the Town and Castle of Stirling, 1835

Stirling owes much of its early prominence and prosperity to the beautiful and picturesque Stirling Old Bridge, which for centuries was the only roadway over the Forth and the most strategically important river crossing in Scotland. The construction of the bridge is ascribed to Robert Duke of Albany, Earl of Fife and Menteith. The bridge, protected by the castle, is the main reason for Stirling's existence. A bridge, probably in timber, existed at least as early as the thirteenth century.

Above and below: Stirling Old Bridge.

Stirling New Bridge.

The roadway of the bridge is supported on four semicircular arches, none of which have the same width of span. The bridge previously had massive towers with arched gateways at each end. The southern arch of the bridge was cut in 1745, during the Jacobite rebellion, to prevent the Highlanders from crossing into Stirling. The bridge was closed to vehicles in 1834.

The old wooden bridge at Stirling, which was central to the Battle of Stirling Bridge on 11 September 1297, was located around 180 yards upstream from Stirling Old Bridge. The battle was a famous victory for Scotland's national hero, William Wallace, during the First War of Scottish Independence.

When news arrived that the Earl of Surrey was pressing forward at the head of a large English army, Wallace immediately advanced to the Forth, and took up his position along the loop of the Forth in front of the Abbey Craig, where the massive tower reared to his memory now stands. Terms offered by the English leaders having been rejected, they advanced to the attack. A proposal that a portion of the army should cross by the neighbouring ford was not acted on, and the whole line began to advance by the bridge, which was so narrow that only two persons could pass abreast. When about half of the English force had crossed, a body of spearmen, sent by Wallace for the purpose, dashing suddenly forward, gained and took possession of the end of the bridge, and Surrey and the rest of his forces had to stand helplessly by and see their comrades who had crossed attacked and routed by the Scottish army.

Ordnance Gazetteer of Scotland, 1882

At a meeting held in Stirling in October, 1826 it was proposed that a new bridge should be built, as the old one was of little use for traffic. The bridge was afterwards contracted for by Mr Kenneth Mathieson, at a cost of £13,368, and completed by Whitsunday, 1832.

Old Faces, Old Places and Old Stories of Stirling, William Drysdale, 1899

In 1831, the fine new bridge was built, which, from its breadth, massive workmanship, and altogether elegant appearance, reflects great credit on the contractor, Mr Kenneth Mathieson.

The Tourist's Companion Through Stirling, John Forbes, 1848

The New Bridge is a handsome and stately structure, stamped with the impress of solidity and strength, and finished in a style of architecture equally elegant and chaste. The foundation-stone of it was laid with much pride, pomp, and circumstance, with all the usual parade and formality of masonic honours, and amid the greetings of thousands of spectators, on the 8th September, 1831. The building was executed by Mr Mathieson, from a design by Robert Stevenson, Esq. Civil Engineer, and on both these gentlemen the work reflects the highest professional credit.

A New Description of the Town and Castle of Stirling, 1935

Stirling New Bridge is just downstream from the Old Bridge. It was opened in 1832 and was designed by Robert Stevenson (1772–1850), one of Scotland's most eminent civil engineers, renowned designer of lighthouses and the grandfather of Robert Louis Stevenson. An alternative design by Thomas Telford was rejected.

44. Raploch Community Campus, Drip Road

Nestling under the highest part of Stirling Castle rock, the village of Raploch enjoys an excellent situation. For many years the majority of the inhabitants were engaged in connection with weaving, and the male portion also vied with each other in the matter of cottage gardening, some of the front plots to the houses being especially pleasurable to behold. After the decay of handloom weaving, quite a different class occupied the village, which went locally by the name *Little Ireland* for a time, and the dirt and squalor were considerable. Now, however, with the introduction of gas and water, considerable improvement has taken place.

Auld Biggins of Stirling, William Drysdale, 1904

Raploch Community Campus.

When I first saw the Raploch it was a pretty place, with flower-beds in front and well-kept gardens in the rear of the houses. Many of the inhabitants were weavers, and the loomshop was on one side, and the dwelling-house on the other side of the entry, some six or eight such shops being situated at the north end of the village. When next I saw it the loomshops had become bedrooms, and the beams of the looms had been turned into bedposts, the beds being covered with haps stolen from the Deanston Works carts as they passed on their way to or from Glasgow. The place had become an Irish colony of the lowest cast.

Old Faces, Old Places and Old Stories of Stirling, William Drysdale, 1899

The landmark Raploch Community Campus, which opened in 2009, is a new civic building that provides facilities for a diverse range of local community services: three schools, a nursery, sports halls, a library and meeting rooms. The cutting-edge building was central to the transformation of the area, which for many years had a negative image. The community-led regeneration project for the area has resulted in the construction of hundreds of new homes and the creation of attractive civic spaces.

45. Airthrey Castle

Airthrey Castle is rich in natural beauty, in a part of the country where picturesque scenery abounds. The entrance to the park of Airthrey is at the distance of two miles from the town of Stirling, and its woods and pleasure-grounds skirt the road from

Stirling to Kinross for a mile and a half. The scenery within the park gates combines a singular variety of beauty, undulating rivers, noble woods, a large artificial piece of water, so managed as to have all the effects of a natural lake; and, above all, precipitous and most picturesque rocky hills, richly wooded and affording a great extent of the most pleasant walks. These grounds possess innumerable points of view which command the most glorious prospects, particularly of Stirling Castle, and the valley of the Firth.

> *The Seats and Arms of the Noblemen and Gentlemen of*
> *Great Britain and Ireland,*
> Sir Bernard Burke, 1855

Records of the Airthrey Estate date back to the twelfth century and over the centuries it passed through the ownership of a number of noble families. In 1759, the estate was sold to the Haldane family who commissioned the landscaping of the grounds by Thomas White and a new house by Robert Adam, which, despite later additions, still forms the core of the present building.

The castle functioned as a maternity hospital during the Second World War and continued in this use until 1969, allowing a number of locals of a certain age to quite correctly claim that they were born in a castle. The Airthrey Estate now forms the campus of the University of Stirling.

Airthrey Castle.

Airthrey Castle.

46. The National Wallace Monument, Abbey Craig

It took a long time for a fitting memorial to be built to Wallace, but when this great landmark was built its grandeur more than compensated for the delay. From the 1820s onwards, proposals had been made for different sites in both Edinburgh and Glasgow for a monument to Wallace. In 1859, the site at Abbey Craig was agreed. A fundraising campaign was established and a national competition organised for a suitable design. John T. Rochead's (1814–78) soaring Scottish Baronial tower surmounted by an imperial crown was the winning entry.

The Scottish Baronial style was a nineteenth-century revival of Scottish architectural forms taking its inspiration from the buildings of the Scottish Renaissance. It is typified by the incorporation of architectural features associated with Scottish castles such as crenellations, turreted bartizans, oriels, and the use of massive hewn stone. One of the motivations behind its development was a revived interest in the exploration of national identity. A romantic image of Scotland had developed around the novels of Sir Walter Scott and the adoption of Scottish Baronial architecture seemed to express the Scottish national identity and tradition. It was, therefore, considered the architectural style which was most appropriate to celebrate one of Scotland's national heroes.

Above left and right: National Wallace Monument.

Below: View from Abbey Craig.

The foundation stone was laid by the Duke of Athole, Grand-Master Mason, amongst much ceremony and in front of a crowd estimated at 80,000 on 24 June 1861. The monument opened on 11 September 1869, the 572nd anniversary of Wallace's great victory at Stirling Bridge.

> In our estimation it would be impossible to find a situation in all respects more suited for a national monument, or better adapted for a memorial cairn to the national hero. Abbey Craig is geographically in the centre of Scotland; it is likewise the centre of the Scottish battle-ground for civil and religious liberty. It overlooks the field of Stirling Bridge, where Wallace obtained his greatest victory; and the monument will surmount the spot where he is believed to have stood while surveying the legions of England crossing the bridge, in their path to destruction.
>
> Revd Dr. Rogers, extract from brochure published in 1861 on the opening of the National Wallace Monument

> Here we feel elevated, as if by enchantment, in the midst of a fairy scene, a panorama of the most ennobling character. Around is a level plain, watered by the silvery courses of the river Forth and guarded at almost every point by stupendous mountains. For miles on every side, everything is picturesque, beautiful, or sublime, there being not one single feature to mar the loveliness of the landscape or detract from the poetry of the scene.
>
> *A Week at Bridge of Allan*, Revd Dr Rogers, 1853

There is a spectacular panorama from Abbey Craig towards Stirling, with the 'silvery Forth reposing, serpent like, in the centre of the plain'. The fertile soil in the meanders or links of the Forth at Stirling gave rise to the old rhyme: 'A crook o' the Forth is worth an Earldom o' the north.'

47. Cambuskenneth Abbey

> The minster (at Cambuskenneth) was 178 feet long and 37 feet broad; it consisted of a nave, with only a single north aisle; a choir and a transept, with an east aisle; their foundations remain, with those of the chapter-house and refectory. The massive detached tower of four stories, Early English, 35 feet square, remains, with the west doorway of the nave in a wall. The site of this solitary tower is most beautiful, almost surrounded by the windings of the Forth, and fine trees; whilst the grand elevation of Stirling on its commanding height, with many spires, a castle, and the steeple of the Grey Friars Church on the south, and the wooded Abbey Crag on the east (now disfigured by the Wallace monument),

Above and right:
Cambuskenneth Abbey.

partly frame the view. Many interesting associations pleaded for its preservation. In 1308, the barons swore at the high altar to defend the title of Robert Bruce. The first Scottish Parliament, with representatives of the cities and burghs, was assembled within the convent walls. Edward I was here November 1, 1303, and March 5, 1304. In 1326, Richard II of England is said to have died a prisoner in Stirling Castle, after a captivity of eighteen years, and probably worshipped here;

and in the same year the National Assembly swore fealty to the line of Bruce, in the presence of King Robert, who came to witness the marriage of his sister Christian to Murray of Bothwell. James III, who died June 11, 1488, and Queen Margaret of Denmark were buried here, and her Majesty Queen Victoria erected a tomb to their memory in 1865.

The Ancient Church of Scotland, Mackenzie Walcott, 1874

We have authentic data that the Abbey of Cambuskenneth was built in the year 1147, and founded by King David I. It was situated in a most pleasant and fertile peninsula of the Forth, about one mile east of the town. Many of the ecclesiastics of this Abbey were remarkable for their piety and learning. Few vestiges of the houses of the ancient ecclesiastics can now be traced out. The only remnant that exists entire is the belfry tower, a portion of the garden, a burying-ground, and a considerable extent of the foundation walls. This Abbey was richly endowed for a religious fraternity of St Augustine, or canons regular, and called the monastery of Stirling, and was dedicated to St Mary.

The Tourist's Companion Through Stirling, John Forbes, 1848

Cambuskenneth Abbey was established by David I in 1147 for canons brought from Aroise Abbey, in Artois, as a dedication to the Virgin Mary. It was originally known as the Abbey of St Mary or the Abbey of Stirling. It was one of the wealthiest and most important abbeys in Scotland due to its royal connections and proximity to Stirling Castle. At its height the abbey comprised an extensive complex of buildings.

The abbey's closeness to Stirling Castle put it in the way of attack during the Wars of Independence – in 1383 it was largely destroyed by the army of King Richard III and it was rebuilt during the early 1400s. It was also the scene of a number of significant historic events, such as in 1314 when King Robert I held a parliament at the abbey following the Battle of Bannockburn.

The abbey was abandoned in 1559 during the Scottish Reformation with stone removed for building work in the town, including Mar's Wark.

The abbey is reduced to its foundations with the exception of the dramatic three-storey square bell tower, which dates from 1300 and is considered to be the finest surviving medieval bell tower in Scotland.

The elaborate tomb on the site marks the last resting place of James III who was murdered near Bannockburn after fleeing the Battle of Sauchieburn on 11 June 1488. He was interred in front of the high altar of the abbey church, alongside his queen, Margaret of Denmark, who died in 1486. The tomb was paid for by Queen Victoria, following the discovery, in 1865, of two coffins which were presumed to be those of the royal couple.

48. St Ninians Old Parish Kirk and St Ninian's Tower, Kirk Wynd

St Ninians is an ancient village approximately a mile south of the centre of Stirling. It developed around the kirk, which is first recorded in the mid-twelfth century. St Ninians prospered in the eighteenth and nineteenth centuries based on local weaving, mining and nail making. After the Second World War, large-scale demolition and road building resulted in the loss of many historic buildings in the village.

There are records of a church on the site in St Ninians from as early as 1150. The church was extensively altered and rebuilt in the early eighteenth century and the classically influenced landmark tower was built in 1734. However, the church was mainly destroyed on 1 January 1746, when it was blown up by the retreating Jacobite army, which had been using the building as a gunpowder magazine. Only the tower and fragments of the church, a fifteenth-century pillar from the original nave, and the sixteenth-century chancel survived the blast.

St Ninian's Tower.

49. Battle of Bannockburn Visitor Centre

The innovative new Battle of Bannockburn Visitor Centre opened on 1 March 2014, in the 700th anniversary year of the battle. The competition-winning design was by Scottish architecture firm Reiach & Hall and the project was managed by the National Trust for Scotland in association with Historic Scotland. In addition to the new visitor centre, the project also involved the repair and restoration of the main battlefield monuments and improvements to the landscape setting. The new visitor centre replaced an earlier facility which dated from the 1960s.

The textured grey-brick walls and austere geometric lines of the building reflect traditional Scottish rural architectural forms and the pattern of the brickwork hints at the appearance of chain mail. The light and airy interior is arranged around a central courtyard with a café area and shop. The main focus is the state-of-the-art immersive displays of the battle, which was a critical event in the history of Scotland.

> Bruce and de Bohun, were fightin' for the croon
> Bruce taen his battle-axe and knocked de Bohun doon.

King Robert was ill mounted, carrying a battle-axe, and, on his bassinet-helmet, wearing, for distinction, a crown. Thus externally distinguished, he rode before the lines, regulating their order, when an English knight, who was ranked amongst the bravest in Edward's army, Sir Henry de Boun, came galloping furiously up to him, to engage him in single combat, expecting, by this act of chivalry, to end the contest and gain immortal fame. But the enterprising champion, having missed his blow, was instantly struck dead by the king, the handle of whose axe was broken with the violence of the shock.

History of Stirlingshire, William Nimmo, 1880

The Battle of Bannockburn, on 23 and 24 June 1314, was a famous victory for the Scots against the vastly superior invading army of King Edward II. The victory secured Robert the Bruce's reputation as one of the great heroes of Scottish history and Scotland's future as an independent nation.

Tradition has it that the Scottish Standard at Bannockburn was raised on a circular millstone, which is known as the Borestone. It became an emblem of national pride for many Scots and a target for early memento hunters who chipped off parts of the stone as keepsakes. The stone was later protected by an iron grille and, in 2014, the remaining two pieces were moved inside the new visitor centre. The original site of the Borestone is marked by a bronze B-shaped plaque.

The flagpole at the site was erected in 1870 by the Dumbarton Loyal Dixon Lodge of the Independent Order of Oddfellows. The rotunda that surrounds the cairn and flagpole includes lines from Kathleen Jamie's poem, 'Here Lies Our Land'.

The bronze equestrian statue of Bruce at Bannockburn, by the sculptor Charles d'Orville Pilkington Jackson, was unveiled in 1964 by Her Majesty The Queen on the 65oth anniversary of the Battle of Bannockburn.

Above and below: Battle of Bannockburn Visitor Centre.

Bruce statue.

5c. Bannockburn House

Bannockburn House dates from around 1675 and was commissioned by Sir Hugh Paterson after he bought the estate from the Rollo family. It is an impressive example of an early grand mansion house, which has survived largely intact. The overall design is influenced by classical architecture, but the inclusion of traditional features, such as crow-stepped gables, cleverly reflects its Scottish ancestry. The house retains some noteworthy seventeenth-century interior detail, including two elaborate decorative plaster ceilings and wall panelling. It is part of a small country estate complete with a seventeenth-century doocot and gate piers, and a nineteenth-century coach house, which contribute to the overall setting of the house.

Charles Edward Stuart, Bonnie Prince Charlie, was a visitor to the house in 1745 before his incursion into England and the prince used the house as his headquarters in 1746 at the time of the Battle of Falkirk Muir. Charles was allegedly shot at through an open window during his stay and met Clementine Walkinshaw, who was to become his mistress, at the house.

In 1884, the house was altered by the new owner, Alexander Wilson, the local weaving magnate. The alterations included the addition of the projecting porch entrance.

The house changed hands a number of times in the twentieth century and, in 2017, it was purchased by a trust with the aim of restoring the property for the long-term benefit of the local community.

Above and below: Bannockburn House.

Acknowledgements

I understand that the correct demonym (it seems that demonym is a word that identifies residents of a particular place) for people from Stirling is Stirlinger. Anyway, a number of Stirlingers took time to offer advice as I was taking photos or having a break in one of the many fine refreshment establishments in the city. This gave the lasting impression that Stirling is a friendly and welcoming place.

Particular thanks to Greg McDougall, David Leslie and Francis Newton for advice and invaluable help with images. My brother, Alastair, knows Stirling very well and was a regular source of encouragement. As ever, I owe an enormous debt of thanks to Emma Jane for her constant patience, support and cups of tea.